Will Shortz Presents

CRAZY FOR KENKEN KILLER

KenKen: Logic Puzzles That Make You Smarter

Will Shortz Presents KenKen Easiest, Volume 1
Will Shortz Presents KenKen Easy, Volume 2
Will Shortz Presents KenKen Easy to Hard, Volume 3
Will Shortz Presents The Little Gift Book of KenKen
Will Shortz Presents Crazy for KenKen Easy
Will Shortz Presents Crazy for KenKen Easy to Hard
Will Shortz Presents Crazy for KenKen Killer

KenKen for Kids

Will Shortz Presents I Can KenKen! Volume 1
Will Shortz Presents I Can KenKen! Volume 2
Will Shortz Presents I Can KenKen! Volume 3

WILL SHORTZ PRESENTS

CRAZY FOR KENKEN™ KILLER

100 LOGIC PUZZLES THAT MAKE YOU SMARTER

TETSUYA MIYAMOTO

INTRODUCTION BY

WILL SHORTZ

ST. MARTIN'S GRIFFIN
NEW YORK

 Printed in the United States of America. For information, address St. Martin's Press, 175 Fifth Avenue, New York, N.Y. 10010.

www.stmartins.com

ISBN-13: 978-0-312-54638-0
ISBN-10: 0-312-54638-6

10 9 8 7 6 5

Introduction

If you consider all the world's greatest puzzle varieties, the ones that have inspired crazes over the years—crosswords, jigsaw puzzles, tangrams, sudoku, etc.—they have several properties in common. They . . .

- Are simple to learn
- Have great depth
- Are variable in difficulty, from easy to hard
- Are mentally soothing and pleasing
- Have some unique feature that makes them different from everything else and instantly addictive

By these standards, a new puzzle called KenKen, the subject of the book you're holding, has the potential to become one of the world's greats.

KenKen is Japanese for "square wisdom" or "cleverness squared." The rules are simple: Fill the grid with digits so as not to repeat a digit in any row or column (as in sudoku) and so the digits within each heavily outlined group of boxes combine to make the arithmetic result indicated.

The simplest KenKen puzzles start with 3×3 boxes and use only addition. Harder examples have larger grids and more arithmetic operations.

KenKen was invented in 2003 by Tetsuya Miyamoto, a Japanese math instructor, as a means to help his students learn arithmetic and develop logical thinking. Tetsuya's education method is unusual. Put simply, he doesn't teach. His philosophy is to make the tools of learning available to students and then let them progress on their own.

Tetsuya's most popular learning tool has been KenKen, which his students spend hours doing and find more engaging than TV and video games.

It's true that KenKen has great capacity for educating and building the mind. But first and foremost it's a puzzle to be enjoyed. It is to numbers what the crossword puzzle is to words.

So turn the page and begin. . . .

—Will Shortz

How to Solve KenKen

KenKen is a logic puzzle with simple rules:

- Fill the grid with digits so as not to repeat a digit in any row or column.
- Digits within each heavily outlined group of squares, called a cage, must combine to make the arithmetic result indicated.
- A 3×3–square puzzle will use the digits from 1 to 3, a 4×4–square puzzle will use the digits from 1 to 4, etc.

Solving a KenKen puzzle involves pure logic and mathematics. No guesswork is needed. Every puzzle has a unique solution.

In this volume of KenKen, the puzzles use all four arithmetic operations—addition, subtraction, multiplication, and division—in the following manner:

- In a cage marked with a plus sign, the given number will be the sum of the digits you enter in the squares.
- In a cage marked with a minus sign, the given number will be the difference between the digits you enter in the squares (the lower digit subtracted from the higher one).

Take the 5×5–square example on this page.

48×		3+		4−
	8+	10×	4+	
3−				2÷
	4+		4	
7+			15×	

To start, fill in any digits in 1×1 sections—in this puzzle, the 4 in the fourth row. These are literally no-brainers.

Next, look for sections whose given numbers are either high or low, or that involve distinctive combinations of digits, since these are often the easiest to solve. For example, the L-shaped group in the upper left has a product of 48. The only combination of three digits from 1 to 5 that multiplies to 48 is 3, 4, and 4. Since the two 4s can't appear in the same row or column, they must appear at the ends of the L. The 3 goes between them.

Now look at the pair of squares in the first row with a sum of 3. The only two digits that add up to 3 are 1 and 2. We don't know their order yet, but this information can still be useful.

Sometimes, the next step in solving a KenKen puzzle is to ignore the given numbers and use sudoku-like logic to avoid repeating a digit in a row or column. For example, now that 1, 2, 3, and 4 have been used or are slated for use in the first row, the remaining square (at the end of the row) must be a 5. Then the digit below the 5 must be a 1 for this pair of squares to have a difference of 4.

Next, consider the pair of squares in the third column with a product of 10. The only two digits from 1 to 5 that have a product of 10 are 2 and 5. We don't know their order yet. However, the digit in the square above them, which we previously identified as either a 1 or a 2, must be 1, so as not to repeat a 2 in this column. The 2 that accompanies the 1 goes to its right.

Continuing in this way, using these and other techniques left for you to discover, you can work your way around the grid, filling in the rest of the squares. The complete solution is shown on page ix.

<table>
<tr><td>48× 3</td><td>4</td><td>3+ 1</td><td>2</td><td>4− 5</td></tr>
<tr><td>4</td><td>8+ 5</td><td>10× 2</td><td>4+ 3</td><td>1</td></tr>
<tr><td>3− 2</td><td>3</td><td>5</td><td>1</td><td>2÷ 4</td></tr>
<tr><td>5</td><td>4+ 1</td><td>3</td><td>4 4</td><td>2</td></tr>
<tr><td>7+ 1</td><td>2</td><td>4</td><td>15× 5</td><td>3</td></tr>
</table>

Additional Tips

- In advanced KenKen puzzles, as you've seen, cages can have more than two squares. It's okay for a cage to repeat a digit—as long as the digit is not repeated in a row or column.
- Cages with more than two squares will always involve addition or multiplication. Subtraction and division occur only in cages with exactly two squares.
- Remember, in doing KenKen, you never have to guess. Every puzzle can be solved by using step-by-step logic. Keep going, and soon you'll be a KenKen master!

Kids can KENKEN™ too!
Will Shortz Presents the Logic Puzzles That Make Math Fun!
Introduction by Marilyn Burns
Will Shortz Presents
I Can KENKEN!!™
75 PUZZLES FOR HAVING FUN WITH MATH
Created by Tetsuya Miyamoto
VOLUME 1 USING ADDITION ONLY
VOLUME 2 USING MULTIPLICATION ONLY
VOLUME 3 USING ADDITION AND SUBTRACTION
St. Martin's Griffi
www.KenKen.com • www.StMartins.co

Easy

÷/×/−/+ **1**

3÷	11+		24×		
	4	3+		11+	
4	25×	6×	5−	2÷	2÷
3÷	24×	6	8+	4−	5+

2 +/−/×/÷ **Easy**

2÷		3÷	25×		3÷
3−				4	
3÷	5−		2÷		5
	25×	11+			12+
		4	2÷	3÷	
4	7+				

Easy ÷/×/−/+ **3**

6	3÷		1−		6×
3+	17+		4−		
			3÷	6+	5
1−		11+			
8+	5+		5−		96×
			3		

4 +/−/×/÷ Easy

1−		4−	6	3÷	1−
4−			2÷		
1−	5−			11+	5+
	2÷	15×			
3÷		3	6+	24×	
	12×			3−	

Easy

÷/×/−/+

5

6	5−	1−		3−	
3+		2÷	25×		1−
	80×		4×		
				2÷	
8+		1	2−	2−	
30×				5−	

6 +/−/×/÷ **Easy**

5	90×	2−	2÷		9+
2−			13+		
		2×		50×	
10+					6
		25×		3−	
36×				5+	

Easy

÷/×/−/+ **7**

25×		4	9×	12+	
5−		13+			
	2÷		1−	2÷	2÷
9+					
	3÷		2−		25×
	2÷		2		

8 +/−/×/÷ Easy

15+	7+		5×	80×	
13+		2÷		3	10+
		120×	3÷		
24×				5−	
		60×			3

Easy ÷/×/−/+ **9**

1−	5−		2	1−	
	15×		5−	1−	
2÷				5−	11+
5	2÷		12+		
5−	6			40×	3÷
	1−				

10 +/−/×/÷ Moderate

36×	180×		3−	5−	
				5+	
	5−		4	30×	1−
	40×	11+			
		2÷			5+
	2÷		5−		

Moderate

÷/×/−/+ **11**

60×		5−		7+	
	3−	2−		2÷	2−
6+		8+	2÷		
				180×	
7+	6+				5
	1−		8×		

12 +/−/×/÷ Moderate

1−	6×	2÷		2	3−
		3	7+	1−	
4−	3+				2÷
	1−		3÷		
36×		11+		2÷	
		2÷		1−	

Moderate

÷/×/−/+ **13**

1−		10+		2÷	
2−			13+	1−	12×
5−		16×			
1−				75×	
	7+	3−	7+		6
				6×	

14 +/−/×/÷ **Moderate**

4−		2÷		9+	2−
20×	13+				
	12+		13+		5−
36×		3+			
			17+		2÷
	4−				

Moderate

÷/×/−/+ **15**

6	2−		8+	4×	
11+		1−			
3+			3	1−	10+
2−		144×			
3÷	40×				
			14+		

16 +/−/×/÷ Moderate

60×			3÷		3−
1−	1−		30×		
	10+			5−	
1−			11+	4	8+
	3−			10+	
2÷		5+			

Moderate

÷/×/−/+

17

1−		12+	360×		2
3−			6+		
	3÷	1−		13+	
4					
6×		120×		120×	
	1−				

18 +/−/×/÷ **Hard**

3÷		60×		3÷	
8+			24×		1−
	2÷	1−			
14+		10+		4−	
		2÷		1−	1−
2−		4−			

Hard ÷/×/−/+ **19**

30×	2−		1−		6
		11+	2	4−	2÷
12+					
		4−	12+		2−
24×	1−		36×		
				3÷	

20 +/−/×/÷ Hard

11+			24×	6	8+
2−	36×				
		16+		6×	
2÷				12×	
2÷	2÷	9+			15+

Hard ÷/×/−/+ **21**

4×		14+			13+
	1−		2÷		
360×	3−			1−	
	144×	9+			4
			15+		
		1−			

22 +/−/×/÷ Hard

5−	12×	5	2÷		9+
		9+		11+	
16+		1−			
1−		10+			12+
	2÷		12+		
2÷		2÷			

Hard

÷/×/−/+ **23**

5	2÷		24×		10+
3−	2÷	1−			
		2	1−		
5+	30×	3−		2÷	1−
		7+	6		
2−				7+	

24 +/−/×/÷ Hard

4−		2−		3÷	40×
17+			24×		
4		2×			
1−				1−	
4−	7+	12+			2−
			1−		

Hard

÷/×/−/+ **25**

2−		1−	10×	1−	
14+				6+	
3		30×	3−	2−	
2÷	5+			3−	
		10+	2÷	1−	7+

26 +/−/×/÷ **Easy**

90×	2÷	5	3+		13+	
		2÷		80×	7×	
	4−					2
11+	11+	13+		3÷	10×	12×
		4×				
6−			2÷		1−	30×
2÷		1−		7		

Easy ÷/×/−/+ 27

7+			4−		11+	
42×	1−		6−		3÷	
	1−		18×		9+	
	2÷	5		20×	6−	
11+		3+			13+	
	6−	13+	4	13+	9×	
4						

28 +/−/×/÷ Easy

24×	4×		3÷		4−	240×
			2−			
140×	3	3÷	7×			
				2÷	11+	1−
3+	11+	2−	2			
			1−	20×	6−	
13+		3			2÷	

Easy

÷/×/−/+

29

6−		3−		1−		7+
12+	2÷		7	16+		
		6−			2÷	
5	16×	72×		49×		5+
			20×	3		
3−		3		2÷	2−	35×
13+		3÷				

30 +/−/×/÷ **Easy**

12×			14×	30×		7
3÷	16+			2×	2−	15×
	2÷					
4−		16+			10+	3+
	3÷		4	2−		
21×	6−		3−		2	2−
	7+			5+		

Easy

÷/×/−/+ **31**

20×		3+		11+		49×
1−	11+	2÷				
			28×			6×
3	210×			4−	14+	
21×		3−				120×
2×	6	42×		2−		
		7				

32 +/−/×/÷ Easy

56×			36×	1−		4−
14+	6−			3+		
		4−		1−		7
	2÷	4	2÷	2−		2÷
28×		25×		6−	6	
	2				5+	3−
4−		1−		4		

Easy

÷/×/−/+ **33**

175×		2÷	3	24×		5−
	3		2−			
1	6×		2÷	2−	1−	
13+	16+				9×	
	13+		2×		7+	
		2−	2−			9+
2÷				3−		

34 +/−/×/÷ Easy

4−	2÷	1−		2−		7
		6−		16+	2	8+
3+		2−				
28×		2÷		36×	5×	
2−		7+				48×
2−	4		6−		2−	
	6−		1−			

Moderate

÷/×/−/+

35

42×			2÷	175×	1−	
2÷	1−					1
	6−	90×	4−			7+
2÷			1−		210×	
	2÷		21×	5−		
17+					24×	1−
		3+				

36 +/−/×/÷ Moderate

11+	5+	42×		6	2−	
		1−		2÷	10+	
	5		6−		2÷	
10+		2÷		13+		3−
	5−		24×	2−	2−	
10+		18×				10+
			5	3+		

Moderate ÷/×/−/+ 37

60×	5	3−		14×	13+	
	2÷	2−				
		3÷	14+	1−	28×	
6×						16+
6×		3÷		5		
	20+		11+		15×	1−
		2÷				

38 +/−/×/÷ **Moderate**

2÷		280×	6−	21+		
36×					24×	
20×			3−			14+
			540×	3÷		
84×		252×		14×		
1−						2
				20×		

Moderate

÷/×/−/+ **39**

3÷		84×		5	72×	11+
3−			6×			
42×	2÷			4−		6+
	9+		3−		5−	
11+			1−			
3−	3−		15+	3÷		30×
	5+					

40 +/−/×/÷ Moderate

6+		28×		2÷		10+
13+			3−	21+		
2÷		3÷			2−	
2÷					3−	35×
1−		21+	6−			
210×				2÷	3÷	1−
		6+				

Moderate

÷/×/−/+ **41**

3÷	14+			126×		
		10×		14+	2−	
2−	3+				5−	2−
	2÷		13+			
1−		13+		13+	11+	
21+		10+				3
					2÷	

42 +/−/×/÷ Moderate

3÷	6−	840×			7+	
		15×		40×		5−
1−					42×	
4−		3−	3÷	5		3−
6+				1−		
20×	2−	3÷	4−		6+	
			8+		6×	

Hard

÷/×/−/+ **43**

12+	2÷		18×			7
		56×		7+	5−	
1−					105×	
3	1−	2−	3÷			
6−			2−		6+	2÷
	12×	12+	5			
				7	1−	

44 +/−/×/÷ Hard

2−		20×	11+		8+	3
4−	36×		15+			2÷
		1−		6+		
1−				60×		
	13+	4−		1−	2÷	2−
1−		2÷				
		3÷		6	5−	

Hard

÷/×/−/+ **45**

4−		48×	2÷		5−	
3−			1−		2−	
2−			2÷		6−	
11+			14+		7+	5
42×		7+				
1−	3−	70×		6+	2÷	2−

46 +/−/×/÷ Hard

10+		2−	17+		2×	
11+				2÷		
1−	14+	1−		4−	4−	1−
			90×			
2−	8+				12+	1−
	36×					
2÷			105×			

Hard

÷/×/−/+ **47**

6−		16×	2÷		3−	
18+			12+		2÷	
		2		19+		3÷
108×		35×	6−			
				12+	1−	1−
	14+					
3−		1−			1−	

48 +/−/×/÷ **Hard**

6×	5−	4	3−	18+		
		1−		7+	2−	1−
5−			1−			
3−	15×			4	60×	
		1−	11+			
30×			7+	4−	3−	
	3−				3÷	

Hard ÷/×/−/+ **49**

2−		9+	1−		30×	10+
2÷			35×			
3−		105×	2÷			
7+	6−			2−	15+	
		24×			11+	
12+			1−			
	10×		3÷		24×	

50 +/−/×/÷ Hard

8+	3−		24×	8+		3÷
	1−				168×	
13+	4−					6+
	3−	19+	5−		5+	
				3−		13+
1−	3÷	8+				
			2−		12+	

Easy

÷/×/−/+ **51**

2÷	30×		9+	6−	15+	2÷	
	1					12×	90×
4−	72×		7	4÷			
		15+		1−	4×		
15+	2÷	11+				7	4×
		3÷	1−		90×		
5−			3÷	2−		2−	
2÷		8				2−	

52 +/−/×/÷ Easy

3+	9+	20×	288×		7	36×	
			3−		7−		
2÷	18×	8		4−	4−		1−
			4		1−	4−	
2−		2÷		7+			4÷
2÷	7−		15+		1−		
	3	17+		4×		9+	
5			10+			7−	

Easy

÷/×/−/+ **53**

7+	21×	2÷		1−		8	6×
		224×	2−		4×		
1−	4−			64×			14+
		25×	3÷				
7−			12×		10+		280×
	4−	2÷			7		
5−		7	4÷		90×		
	5−		8	9+		1−	

54 +/−/×/÷ Easy

21+		15+	6×	18×		2÷	5−
18+							
			80×		49×	3	5−
2÷	12+						
		28×		1−	20×	3÷	3
2÷		7−					20×
8+	2	9+	13+		3−		
			3	11+		7−	

Easy ÷/×/−/+ 55

7	3+		20×	1−	2÷		24×
3÷	15+				75×		
		2÷		5×			3÷
13+		3−	3÷			7	
48×				168×	7−		7
		21×				10+	40×
4−	1−		3	2÷			
		6	4−		4÷		

56 +/−/×/÷ Easy

15×	8+	2÷		1−	15+	5−	
		4−	8			2−	
6+			8+	2÷		48×	
2÷	36×			15+	10+		7
	128×		9+			4−	1−
84×				12×	3		
		4−			6×	160×	
6×		2−				7	

Easy

÷/×/−/+ **57**

15×	15+	96×		3÷	6+	2÷	
		4				336×	
4÷	10+	15+			10+		
			3÷	2÷	5−	4−	
9+						3−	
17+		3+	3−		2÷		2
4			35×	7−		12+	
3÷				7	24×		

58 +/−/×/÷ Easy

2−		2÷	12+		3+		10+
4−			17+		10×		
18+		8				4÷	
	6+	11+	4÷		3	90×	
2÷			2×	48×			4
	10+				210×	2−	
3÷		2÷	2−			2−	11+
	7			2÷			

Easy

÷/×/−/+

59

13+			2−	2−	1−	4×	
1−	15+					7+	
	19+			3+			2−
2−		8	3+	42×			
49×		60×		64×	90×		
	3+		4			2÷	
11+			13+		4	4÷	
	4	3÷		7+		1−	

60 +/−/×/÷ Moderate

4−		8	14+	3÷		84×	
15+							6−
12+		2÷	4−		18+		
3÷			7+	560×			11+
17+	2÷				7−		
		49×				16+	
	672×		3	5×	12+		
						2÷	

Moderate

÷/×/−/+ **61**

1−	2−	2÷		4−		2−	
		192×	10+	3+	35×	7−	
6−						480×	3−
	10+						
13+		7+		19+		84×	6−
3+		210×					
168×		80×			6−		1−
				5	6×		

62 +/−/×/÷ Moderate

2−		7−	14+	2÷		2−	
3÷	4−				35×	2÷	80×
		1−					
40×		72×	64×		42×		
				2−			8+
40×	3−		17+		7−	2÷	
	6×		2−				10+
8+		5			4−		

Moderate

÷/×/−/+ **63**

5−		2÷		4−		2÷	
1−	7−	84×	10+		7+	17+	
							20+
2÷			16+	288×		24×	
1−					5−		
96×	1−		6−				
		36×			5	49×	7−
30×			2−				

64 +/−/×/÷ Moderate

11+	21+				18+		16×
	15+		2−				
		90×	56×			42×	
1−	2−			3+	7−		
		3−			16+	13+	4÷
4	6×	4−	2÷	2−			
4÷						4−	1−
		6×		4			

Moderate

÷/×/−/+ **65**

2240×					14+	108×	
84×			2			15+	
1−		1−		20+			
7−	3+		12+		2÷		
	15+				28×		2÷
4−		2−		10+			
		2÷	7−	2−		7+	1−
3+				10+			

66 +/−/×/÷ Moderate

18+	2÷		4	7−	8+		4−
	256×		25×		13+		
				1−		16×	
	14+		24+		3−		4
1−		14×				48×	
			18+		5−		
7−	20+				6−		4−
			1−		1−		

Moderate

÷/×/−/+ **67**

5−	2−	15+	2−		3÷		9+
			2÷		19+		
48×	3−		9×			3+	18+
	224×				16+		
			10+				
6+		2÷		2÷	7	2÷	
13+		4−	15+		5−	5−	
	3					28×	

68 +/−/×/÷ Hard

11+	3÷		23+		40×		1
	48×		4−				5−
		56×		210×			
17+			3÷	4−	7−		24×
7−		15×			12×		
	2		13+			960×	1−
2−	9+		17+				
				1−			

Hard

÷/×/−/+ **69**

21+			120×	2−		4−	
11+				12+		2÷	2−
		21+					
12+	1−		12×		1−	12×	
		1−				80×	
14+	4÷		11+		6−		15+
		5−					
2÷		15×			336×		

70 +/−/×/÷ Hard

9+	1−	4÷	12+		24×		11+
			30×			2÷	
1−	14+			1−			4−
			7−		3−	49×	
2÷		64×					
2−		48×		24×	2−		2−
20+	5−		2÷		4−		
						6−	

Hard

÷/×/−/+ **71**

2−		11+		2−		2÷	
140×		4÷		192×	3×		7+
	168×	3÷	15+				
					16+		
14+	2÷			3−	1−	15+	
	3÷					22+	
2÷	11+	11+		168×	4−		
						4−	

72 +/−/×/÷ Hard

8+	6×		2−		18+		4−
	60×			2÷			
11+	8×		4−		2−	6−	
	6−		2−			2÷	
		7−		5−	80×		10+
3−		3−				2÷	
144×	56×		40×		42×		6+
		10+					

Hard

÷/×/−/+ **73**

18+		2÷		12+		144×	
	5−	240×			7+		
3−		48×	1−	16×	280×		
							15×
2−		3−	16+		12×		
2−			12+			1−	1−
6	4−			3÷	6−		
4−		1−				4÷	

74 +/−/×/÷ **Hard**

2÷	9+	56×	48×	9+		5−	
				1008×	1−		3
96×	1−				14+		
		1−				3÷	1−
	5	14+		7+	30×		
16+	7−						3−
		2−			8×		
13+			6−		15+		

Hard

÷/×/−/+ **75**

1−	42×		13+	1−	7−		1−
	17+				4−	4−	
1−			1−				12+
	12+	192×		3÷		1−	
2				2÷	3−		96×
30×		4−	7−				
	64×			20+	18+		1−

76 +/−/×/÷ Easy

30×		17+		18+	4÷		7+	3−
3÷	7−				6	35×		
	180×		7−	1−	56×		13+	1
3÷						162×		3−
280×		2−		8−			2	
	8×	3+		45×	7+		18+	
2		3−				3−		
5−	4−	14+	140×			3+		576×
				6	3+			

Easy

÷/×/−/+ **77**

18+		10+		3+		2−	11+	63×
		2	56×		17+			
90×			3+			9	36×	
63×	3−	2÷	3÷	9	30×	3+		
				30×				2÷
15+	8−		2−		112×			
		2−		9×		2−	13+	
2×			72×	11+			8	10×
	1−				4	6−		

78 +/−/×/÷ Easy

6×	7−		9+		800×	8−	4	15+
	63×		60×					
8−	7−					18+		64×
	5−	2÷		13+	7			
3−		14+			5−	1−	4×	
	2−		3÷	8×				315×
17+	6	10+			17+		3÷	
			3÷		1−	7		
1−		1	17+			11+		

Easy

÷/×/−/+ **79**

210×		224×	15+		4÷		9×	
3+				56×	3−			5
	4÷		17+		2−	6×	36×	
13+		17+		5			224×	
	6		36×		8−			
2−				3×	4	3−	4÷	18×
1−		17+	5					
5−			6−	12+		1−	12+	
	3+			2÷			5−	

80 +/−/×/÷ Easy

1−		1−	24×	17+	378×	4÷		13+
1	28×					6−		
3÷		16+				6	8−	
	17+	21×		3−		5×		4
5−		30×	14×	3+			4	189×
	4−				8	16+		
315×		9×	4−		1−			16+
	3÷			1−		48×		
		13+			30×			

Easy

÷/×/−/+ **81**

4−		17+		8+		1−		1−
8−		2−	1−	4÷	6	5−		
8+					15+		64×	
22+	1−	3÷	2−	8−	28×	2÷	9	
							126×	6
	3×		36×	160×				
28×	8				1−	17+	8+	7+
	10+		8−	30×				
2	1−				15×		36×	

82 +/−/×/÷ **Easy**

3+	16+		16+	4÷	270×			4
	12×				3−		8−	
3÷				13+		9	72×	14×
	225×	112×		16×				
		5−			9+		2−	5−
6	14+		9+	3−	10+			
3−		17+			2		7−	
			16+		126×	10×		
4÷		4	8−				1−	

Easy ÷/×/−/+ 83

8−	1−		3+		14+	14+		1−
	8	28×				15×		
3÷	21×		20+	4÷	504×		1−	4÷
	9×					7−		
		2−		7	18+		3÷	3÷
4÷		1	4−	40×				
24×		11+			2÷		2−	5
17+			96×		20+	3		4×
	72×							

84 +/−/×/÷ Easy

105×	2	14+		6×		224×		
	17+		4−			360×	2÷	
	6×		21+		8			10×
7−		3		1−	16+			
	3−		7		1−	3+		216×
13+		17+				7−	6	
1−		3+		48×	21×		270×	
9+	2÷		1−			3÷		
	1−						8+	

Moderate

÷/×/−/+ **85**

11+		360×			1−		2÷	6−
	11+		108×		320×			
8−		1−				28×		5
336×	5−		140×		8−		90×	
		4		1−		5−		
3−	2−		14+	2÷		2÷	216×	
	5−			5−	11+			22+
189×		4−	16×			10+		
					7			

86 +/−/×/÷ Moderate

8+	16+	8	1−		5−	4÷	3−	
		3÷		9+			1−	
13+	25×				1−		13+	144×
	72×		135×	2÷		13+		
2÷				3−				
	4÷	63×		8−		72×		
8			28×		630×		4−	3÷
3−		16×	2−					
54×				21×			3−	

Moderate

÷/×/−/+ **87**

11+		1−		18+		7	18×	
19+	25×		2÷			2−		
		11+		10+		4×	144×	
	17+			3÷				
2÷	8−		30×		5−		9+	
	11+	3÷		10+	120×			1440×
5−		56×			7−		14+	
	5−		2−	2−		9+		
16+				7				

88 +/−/×/÷ Moderate

192×		21+			8−		1−	
	10+		4×	5−		8+		21+
17+				112×		3−		
	30×		13+	9×		84×		
3−							1−	
2÷		1−		1−	270×		4−	
378×		5−				24×	16×	
2−		1	294×	3−				
	4−				1−		8−	

Moderate

÷/×/−/+

89

216×	8−		17+		3−		2−	
	4−	21+		3+		64×	36×	
					12×			
6×		80×	17+			1−		1−
2−	4÷			108×			8+	
		3−		3−		84×		17+
6−	12×	24×		25×			7−	
		3−	8−	9+				4÷
21×					22+			

90 +/−/×/÷ Moderate

15+			3÷		2−	1−	4×
26+		80×					6
		10+			90×		17+
17+	12×		42×	21+	3+		13+
	2÷					6−	7−
1	49×	3−			2÷		14+
			4÷	17+		2−	15×
2÷	3−	4−			14+		
			2÷			1−	

Moderate

÷/×/−/+ **91**

16+	1−	225×		9×	6	2÷		14+
			63×			4−		
	2−			252×	1−	3÷		
3÷	2−	4−				360×		
		4÷			40×	17+		
6−		168×	5−	3÷			12+	8+
2÷					17+			
96×				20×		4−	3−	4−
	192×							

92 +/−/×/÷ Moderate

9	16×	3+		1−		11+		90×
		1−	3−	7−			36×	
1−				10×				
30×		24×		16+	18+			7−
2−		48×	3÷		13+		441×	
					1			
7−		2−		2÷		3−		256×
11+		108×		8−		3−		
	35×			2−			2÷	

Hard

÷/×/−/+ **93**

3÷	40×			2−	24×			3−
	20+	5−			6−	12+		
			8+			3−	4÷	8+
15+		2−		4	360×			
	20+		2÷				2−	3÷
		432×		21×		56×		
3+			11+	2−	10+		3−	8−
20×		3÷						
13+			17+				4÷	

94 +/−/×/÷ Hard

48×		3−		3	45×		26+	
105×	19+	12+		4÷				
			7−		1−	1−		5−
		2−	4÷			3÷		2−
24×	4−		17+			2÷	20×	
		56×		4−				8−
	10×		252×		8+	56×	2−	
2÷		8−						4−
13+			17+			4−		

Hard

÷/×/–/+ **95**

4–	15+	14+			9+		5	15×
		12+		6–		1–		
9	17+		24×		22+	16×		
						4–	1–	5–
2÷	6+	17+		17+				
		3÷			8+		72×	
3840×		27×			4–		1–	
		9×	70×		2–		7+	13+
				1–				

96 +/−/×/÷ Hard

12×		10+	7+	4−		25+	3−	
2÷	14×						14+	
		864×	2÷		7+	2−		3÷
5			3÷			28×		
8−			22+			3−		9+
14+	15×	4÷	14+			2−		
			9	224×		6+		20×
	108×	240×			9+			
			1−			6−		

Hard ÷/×/−/+ 97

30×	17+		16×	8+			42×	
				18+		6	108×	2−
20+	8−			5				
	4−	1−	23+		2÷	2÷		1−
						400×		
39+							3÷	
9+	20+		11+				2−	
			25+		36×		10+	
	2÷				112×			

98 +/−/×/÷ Hard

5−	17+		2÷		11+	27×	42×	
			2÷					2÷
6−		32×	3÷		56×	16+	7	
3−			2−					3÷
7+			21+	216×		18+		
2−	4−						7+	3÷
		2÷		2−	24×			
3−		3−				72×	7−	
1−		21+					6+	

Hard

÷/×/−/+ **99**

11+	2÷	6−		16+		3−	15+	
		360×	3−		12+			7
	672×						24×	
			144×		504×	9+		
24+		9×					3−	
		24×		1400×	22+		1−	
					4÷		2÷	3−
1−		3÷				3÷		
40×		3−		4−			6−	

100 +/−/×/÷ Hard

4−		5−		126×			4÷	13+
17+	21×		20×		15+			
		13+		1−		5+	20×	
4÷			1890×					9
9+	17+				112×	16+		
		17+	36×				4−	
				30×				1−
3÷	2−	6+			4−	2−		
		16+				17+		

ANSWERS

1

3÷ 1	11+ 6	5	24× 4	3	2
3	4 4	3+ 1	2	11+ 6	5
4 4	25× 5	6× 3	5− 1	2÷ 2	2÷ 6
5	1	2	6	4	3
3÷ 2	24× 3	6 6	8+ 5	4− 1	5+ 4
6	2	4	3	5	1

2

2÷ 2	4	3÷ 6	25× 1	5	3÷ 3
3− 6	3	2	5	4 4	1
3÷ 3	5− 6	1	2÷ 4	2	5 5
1	25× 5	11+ 3	2	6	12+ 4
5	1	4 4	2÷ 6	3÷ 3	2
4 4	7+ 2	5	3	1	6

3

6 6	3÷ 3	1	1− 4	5	6× 2
3+ 2	17+ 6	4	4− 5	1	3
1	4	3	3÷ 6	6+ 2	5 5
1− 4	5	11+ 6	2	3	1
8+ 3	5+ 2	5	5− 1	6	96× 4
5	1	2	3 3	4	6

4

1− 5	4	4− 2	6 6	3÷ 1	1− 3
4− 1	5	6	2÷ 4	3	2
1− 3	5− 6	1	2	11+ 5	5+ 4
4	2÷ 2	15× 5	3	6	1
3÷ 2	1	3 3	6+ 5	24× 4	6
6	12× 3	4	1	3− 2	5

5

6 6	5− 1	1− 4	3	3− 2	5
3+ 2	6	2÷ 3	25× 5	1	1− 4
1	80× 4	6	4× 2	5	3
4	5	2	1	2÷ 3	6
8+ 5	3	1 1	2− 6	2− 4	2
30× 3	2	5	4	5− 6	1

6

5 5	90× 3	2− 6	2÷ 2	1	9+ 4
2− 1	5	4	13+ 6	3	2
3	6	2× 1	4	50× 2	5
10+ 4	1	2	3	5	6 6
2	4	25× 5	1	3− 6	3
36× 6	2	3	5	5+ 4	1

7

25× 5	1	4 4	9× 3	12+ 6	2
5− 6	5	13+ 2	1	3	4
1	2÷ 4	6	1− 5	2÷ 2	2÷ 3
9+ 3	2	5	4	1	6
2	3÷ 3	1	2− 6	4	25× 5
4	2÷ 6	3	2 2	5	1

8

15+ 6	7+ 4	3	5× 1	80× 2	5
3	6	1	5	4	2
13+ 1	5	2÷ 4	2	3 3	10+ 6
5	2	120× 6	3÷ 3	1	4
24× 2	3	5	4	5− 6	1
4	1	60× 2	6	5	3 3

9

1− 3	5− 1	6	2 2	1− 5	4
4	15× 5	1	5− 6	1− 3	2
2÷ 2	4	3	1	5− 6	11+ 5
5 5	2÷ 2	4	12+ 3	1	6
5− 1	6 6	5	4	40× 2	3÷ 3
6	1− 3	2	5	4	1

10

36× 2	180× 3	4	3− 5	5− 1	6
6	5	3	2	5+ 4	1
3	5− 6	1	4 4	30× 2	1− 5
1	40× 2	11+ 5	6	3	4
4	1	2÷ 6	3	5	5+ 2
5	2÷ 4	2	5− 1	6	3

11

60× 2	5	5− 6	1	7+ 3	4
6	3− 4	2− 3	5	2÷ 2	2− 1
6+ 5	1	8+ 2	2÷ 6	4	3
1	2	4	3	180× 5	6
7+ 4	6+ 3	1	2	6	5 5
3	1− 6	5	8× 4	1	2

12

1− 5	6× 1	2÷ 6	3	2 2	3− 4
4	6	3 3	7+ 2	1− 5	1
4− 6	3+ 2	1	5	4	2÷ 3
2	1− 5	4	3÷ 1	3	6
36× 3	4	11+ 5	6	2÷ 1	2
1	3	2÷ 2	4	1− 6	5

13

(1−) 6	5	(10+) 3	1	(2÷) 4	2
(2−) 5	3	6	(13+) 2	(1−) 1	(12×) 4
(5−) 1	6	(16×) 4	5	2	3
(1−) 2	4	1	6	(75×) 3	5
3	(7+) 1	(3−) 2	(7+) 4	5	(6) 6
4	2	5	3	(6×) 6	1

14

(4−) 1	5	(2÷) 4	2	(9+) 6	(2−) 3
(20×) 4	(13+) 3	6	1	2	5
5	(12+) 2	3	(13+) 4	1	(5−) 6
(36×) 3	6	(3+) 2	5	4	1
6	4	1	(17+) 3	5	(2÷) 2
2	(4−) 1	5	6	3	4

15

(6) 6	(2−) 3	5	(8+) 2	(4×) 1	4
(11+) 5	6	(1−) 3	4	2	1
(3+) 2	1	4	(3) 3	(1−) 6	(10+) 5
(2−) 4	2	(144×) 6	1	5	3
(3÷) 3	(40×) 5	1	6	4	2
1	4	2	(14+) 5	3	6

16

(60×) 5	4	3	(3÷) 2	6	(3−) 1
(1−) 3	(1−) 5	6	(30×) 1	2	4
4	(10+) 2	5	3	(5−) 1	6
(1−) 1	6	2	(11+) 5	(4) 4	(8+) 3
2	(3−) 1	4	6	(10+) 3	5
(2÷) 6	3	(5+) 1	4	5	2

17

(1−) 3	4	(12+) 1	(360×) 5	6	(2) 2
(3−) 2	5	6	(6+) 1	3	4
5	(3÷) 2	(1−) 4	3	(13+) 1	6
(4) 4	6	3	2	5	1
(6×) 6	1	(120×) 5	4	(120×) 2	3
1	(1−) 3	2	6	4	5

18

(3÷) 1	3	(60×) 4	5	(3÷) 6	2
(8+) 2	1	3	(24×) 6	4	(1−) 5
5	(2÷) 4	(1−) 2	3	1	6
(14+) 3	2	(10+) 6	4	(4−) 5	1
6	5	(2÷) 1	2	(1−) 3	(1−) 4
(2−) 4	6	(4−) 5	1	2	3

19

30× 2	2− 1	3	1− 5	4	6 6
5	3	11+ 6	2 2	4− 1	2÷ 4
12+ 3	6	4	1	5	2
1	2	4− 5	12+ 4	6	2− 3
24× 6	1− 4	1	36× 3	2	5
4	5	2	6	3÷ 3	1

20

11+ 4	5	2	24× 3	6 6	8+ 1
2− 3	36× 1	6	4	2	5
5	6	16+ 4	2	6× 1	3
2÷ 6	3	1	5	12× 4	2
2÷ 1	2÷ 2	9+ 5	6	3	15+ 4
2	4	3	1	5	6

21

4× 4	1	14+ 5	6	3	13+ 2
1	1− 3	4	2÷ 2	6	5
360× 6	3− 5	2	1	1− 4	3
2	144× 6	9+ 1	3	5	4 4
3	4	6	15+ 5	2	1
5	2	1− 3	4	1	6

22

5− 6	12× 4	5 5	2÷ 2	1	9+ 3
1	3	9+ 4	5	11+ 6	2
16+ 5	6	1− 2	1	3	4
1− 3	5	10+ 6	4	2	12+ 1
4	2÷ 2	1	12+ 3	5	6
2÷ 2	1	2÷ 3	6	4	5

23

5 5	2÷ 3	6	24× 2	4	10+ 1
3− 1	2÷ 2	1− 5	4	3	6
4	1	2 2	1− 5	6	3
5+ 3	30× 6	3− 4	1	2÷ 2	1− 5
2	5	7+ 3	6 6	1	4
2− 6	4	1	3	7+ 5	2

24

4− 1	5	2− 6	4	3÷ 3	40× 2
17+ 5	6	3	24× 2	1	4
4 4	3	2× 1	6	2	5
1− 3	4	2	1	1− 5	6
4− 6	7+ 2	12+ 5	3	4	2− 1
2	1	4	1− 5	6	3

25

2− 4	6	1− 3	10× 5	1− 2	1
14+ 6	3	4	2	6+ 1	5
3 3	5	30× 6	3− 1	2− 4	2
2÷ 2	5+ 1	5	4	3− 3	6
1	4	10+ 2	2÷ 6	1− 5	7+ 3
5	2	1	3	6	4

26

90× 3	2÷ 4	5 5	3+ 1	2	13+ 6	7
5	2	2÷ 3	6	80× 4	7× 7	1
6	4− 3	7	4	5	1	2 2
11+ 4	11+ 5	13+ 6	7	3÷ 1	10× 2	12× 3
7	6	4× 1	2	3	5	4
6− 1	7	2	2÷ 3	6	1− 4	30× 5
2÷ 2	1	1− 4	5	7 7	3	6

27

7+ 1	4	2	4− 7	3	11+ 6	5
42× 3	1− 5	4	6− 1	7	3÷ 2	6
7	1− 2	3	18× 6	1	9+ 5	4
2	2÷ 6	5 5	3	20× 4	6− 7	1
11+ 6	3	3+ 1	2	5	13+ 4	7
5	6− 1	13+ 7	4 4	13+ 6	9× 3	2
4 4	7	6	5	2	1	3

28

24× 3	4× 1	4	3÷ 6	2	4− 7	240× 5
4	2	1	2− 5	7	3	6
140× 5	3 3	3÷ 6	7× 7	1	4	2
7	4	2	1	2÷ 6	11+ 5	1− 3
3+ 1	11+ 5	2− 7	2 2	3	6	4
2	6	5	1− 3	20× 4	6− 1	7
13+ 6	7	3 3	4	5	2÷ 2	1

29

6− 1	7	3− 5	2	1− 4	3	7+ 6
12+ 3	2÷ 2	4	7 7	16+ 6	5	1
6	3	6− 7	1	5	2÷ 2	4
5 5	16× 4	72× 2	6	49× 7	1	5+ 3
4	1	6	20× 5	3 3	7	2
3− 2	5	3 3	4	2÷ 1	2− 6	35× 7
13+ 7	6	3÷ 1	3	2	4	5

30

12× 4	1	3	14× 2	30× 6	5	7 7
3÷ 2	16+ 4	5	7	2× 1	2− 6	15× 3
6	2÷ 3	7	1	2	4	5
4− 1	6	16+ 4	5	7	10+ 3	3+ 2
5	3÷ 2	6	4 4	2− 3	7	1
21× 3	6− 7	1	3− 6	5	2 2	2− 4
7	7+ 5	2	3	5+ 4	1	6

31

20× 4	5	3+ 1	2	11+ 3	6	49× 7
1− 5	11+ 4	2÷ 3	6	2	7	1
6	2	5	28× 4	7	1	6× 3
3 3	210× 7	6	5	4− 1	14+ 4	2
21× 7	3	3− 4	1	5	2	120× 6
2× 1	6 6	42× 2	7	2− 4	3	5
2	1	7 7	3	6	5	4

32

56× 2	4	7	36× 3	1− 6	5	4− 1
14+ 6	6− 7	3	4	3+ 2	1	5
5	1	4− 2	6	1− 3	4	7 7
3	2÷ 6	4 4	2÷ 1	2− 5	7	2÷ 2
28× 7	3	25× 5	2	6− 1	6 6	4
4	2 2	1	5	7	5+ 3	3− 6
4− 1	5	1− 6	7	4 4	2	3

33

175× 7	5	2÷ 1	3 3	24× 6	4	5− 2
5	3 3	2	2− 6	4	1	7
1 1	6× 2	3	2÷ 4	2− 5	1− 7	6
13+ 6	16+ 4	5	2	7	9× 3	1
4	13+ 6	7	2× 1	2	7+ 5	3
3	7	2− 6	2− 5	1	2	9+ 4
2÷ 2	1	4	7	3− 3	6	5

34

4− 2	2÷ 6	1− 4	5	2− 1	3	7 7
6	3	6− 1	7	16+ 4	2 2	8+ 5
3+ 1	2	2− 6	4	5	7	3
28× 4	7	2÷ 3	6	36× 2	5× 5	1
2− 7	5	7+ 2	3	6	1	48× 4
2− 3	4 4	5	6− 1	7	2− 6	2
5	6− 1	7	1− 2	3	4	6

35

42× 1	6	7	2÷ 4	175× 5	1− 3	2
2÷ 6	1− 3	4	2	7	5	1 1
3	6− 7	90× 5	4− 6	2	1	7+ 4
2÷ 2	1	6	1− 5	4	210× 7	3
4	2÷ 2	3	21× 7	5− 1	6	5
17+ 5	4	1	3	6	24× 2	1− 7
7	5	3+ 2	1	3	4	6

36

11+ 1	5+ 4	42× 7	2	6 6	2− 3	5
7	1	1− 5	3	2÷ 2	10+ 4	6
3	5 5	6	6− 7	4	2÷ 1	2
10+ 5	3	2÷ 2	1	13+ 7	6	3− 4
2	5− 7	4	24× 6	2− 3	2− 5	1
10+ 6	2	18× 1	4	5	7	10+ 3
4	6	3	5 5	3+ 1	2	7

37

60× 3	5 5	3− 7	4	14× 2	13+ 6	1
4	2÷ 2	2− 5	3	7	1	6
5	4	3÷ 1	14+ 6	1− 3	28× 7	2
6× 6	1	3	7	4	2	16+ 5
6× 2	3	3÷ 6	1	5 5	4	7
1	20+ 7	2	11+ 5	6	15× 3	1− 4
7	6	2÷ 4	2	1	5	3

38

2÷ 2	1	280× 4	6− 7	21+ 5	3	6
36× 3	6	7	1	2	24× 4	5
20× 1	2	5	3− 4	7	6	14+ 3
4	5	2	540× 6	3÷ 3	1	7
84× 7	3	252× 6	5	14× 1	2	4
1− 5	4	1	3	6	7	2 2
6	7	3	2	20× 4	5	1

39

3÷ 3	1	84× 6	2	5 5	72× 4	11+ 7
3− 2	5	7	6× 1	6	3	4
42× 7	2÷ 4	2	6	4− 1	5	6+ 3
6	9+ 3	5	3− 7	4	5− 2	1
11+ 5	6	1	1− 4	3	7	2
3− 1	3− 7	4	15+ 3	3÷ 2	6	30× 5
4	5+ 2	3	5	7	1	6

40

6+ 1	5	28× 7	4	2÷ 3	6	10+ 2
13+ 6	3	4	3− 2	21+ 5	7	1
2÷ 2	1	3÷ 3	5	7	2− 4	6
2÷ 4	2	1	3	6	3− 5	35× 7
1− 3	4	21+ 6	6− 7	1	2	5
210× 5	7	2	6	2÷ 4	3÷ 1	1− 3
7	6	6+ 5	1	2	3	4

41

3÷ 2	14+ 5	1	4	126× 3	7	6
6	4	10× 5	2	14+ 7	2− 3	1
2− 5	3+ 1	2	3	4	5− 6	2− 7
3	2÷ 2	4	13+ 7	6	1	5
1− 4	3	13+ 7	6	13+ 1	11+ 5	2
21+ 1	7	10+ 6	5	2	4	3 3
7	6	3	1	5	2÷ 2	4

42

3÷ 2	6− 1	840× 7	5	6	7+ 4	3
6	7	15× 3	4	40× 2	5	5− 1
1− 3	2	5	1	4	42× 7	6
4− 7	3	3− 1	3÷ 2	5 5	6	3− 4
6+ 1	5	4	6	1− 3	2	7
20× 4	2− 6	3÷ 2	4− 3	7	6+ 1	5
5	4	6	8+ 7	1	6× 3	2

43

12+ 5	2÷ 2	4	18× 1	3	6	7 7
4	3	56× 2	7	7+ 5	5− 1	6
1− 6	7	1	4	2	105× 5	3
3 3	1− 4	2− 5	3÷ 2	6	7	1
6− 1	5	7	2− 6	4	6+ 3	2÷ 2
7	12× 6	12+ 3	5 5	1	2	4
2	1	6	3	7 7	1− 4	5

44

2− 6	4	20× 5	11+ 2	7	8+ 1	3 3
4− 3	36× 6	4	15+ 5	2	7	2÷ 1
7	3	1− 6	4	6+ 1	5	2
1− 1	2	7	6	60× 3	4	5
2	13+ 1	4− 3	7	1− 5	2÷ 6	2− 4
1− 5	7	2÷ 2	1	4	3	6
4	5	3÷ 1	3	6 6	5− 2	7

45

4− 1	5	48× 4	2÷ 3	6	5− 2	7
3− 4	1	2	1− 6	7	2− 5	3
2− 5	3	6	2÷ 4	2	6− 7	1
11+ 6	2	3	14+ 7	4	7+ 1	5 5
42× 7	6	7+ 1	5	3	4	2
1− 2	3− 4	70× 7	1	6+ 5	2÷ 3	2− 6
3	7	5	2	1	6	4

46

10+ 3	7	2− 5	17+ 4	6	2× 1	2
11+ 6	5	3	7	2÷ 2	4	1
1− 1	14+ 4	1− 2	3	4− 5	4− 7	1− 6
2	6	4	90× 5	1	3	7
2− 5	8+ 1	7	6	3	12+ 2	1− 4
7	36× 3	1	2	4	6	5
2÷ 4	2	6	105× 1	7	5	3

47

6− 1	7	16× 4	2÷ 6	3	3− 5	2
18+ 7	4	1	12+ 2	5	2÷ 3	6
4	1	2 2	5	19+ 6	7	3÷ 3
108× 3	6	35× 5	6− 7	2	4	1
6	3	7	1	12+ 4	1− 2	1− 5
2	14+ 5	6	3	7	1	4
3− 5	2	1− 3	4	1	1− 6	7

48

6× 3	5− 2	4 4	3− 1	18+ 6	5	7
2	7	1− 6	4	7+ 5	2− 1	1− 3
5− 6	1	5	1− 7	2	3	4
3− 7	15× 3	1	6	4 4	60× 2	5
4	5	1− 2	11+ 3	1	7	6
30× 5	6	3	7+ 2	4− 7	3− 4	1
1	3− 4	7	5	3	3÷ 6	2

49

2− 4	6	9+ 5	1− 2	1	30× 3	10+ 7
2÷ 6	3	4	35× 7	5	2	1
3− 1	4	105× 7	2÷ 3	6	5	2
7+ 2	6− 7	3	5	2− 4	15+ 1	6
5	1	24× 6	4	2	11+ 7	3
12+ 3	2	1	1− 6	7	4	5
7	10× 5	2	3÷ 1	3	24× 6	4

50

8+ 7	3− 3	6	24× 4	8+ 5	1	3÷ 2
1	1− 5	4	3	2	168× 7	6
13+ 5	4− 7	3	2	6	4	6+ 1
2	3− 4	19+ 7	5− 6	1	5+ 3	5
6	1	5	7	3− 4	2	13+ 3
1− 3	3÷ 2	8+ 1	5	7	6	4
4	6	2	2− 1	3	12+ 5	7

51

2÷ 3	30× 5	6	9+ 2	6− 1	15+ 7	2÷ 8	4
6	1 1	2	5	7	8	12× 4	90× 3
4− 1	72× 6	4	7 7	4÷ 8	2	3	5
5	3	15+ 7	8	1− 2	4× 4	1	6
15+ 8	2÷ 4	11+ 5	6	3	1	7 7	4× 2
7	8	3÷ 3	1− 4	5	90× 6	2	1
5− 2	7	1	3÷ 3	2− 4	5	2− 6	8
2÷ 4	2	8 8	1	6	3	2− 5	7

52

3+ 1	9+ 2	20× 5	288× 6	8	7 7	36× 3	4
2	7	4	3− 5	6	7− 8	1	3
2÷ 4	18× 1	8 8	2	4− 5	4− 3	7	1− 6
8	6	3	4 4	1	1− 5	4− 2	7
2− 7	5	2÷ 2	1	7+ 3	4	6	4÷ 8
2÷ 3	7− 8	1	15+ 7	4	1− 6	5	2
6	3 3	17+ 7	8	4× 2	1	9+ 4	5
5 5	4	6	10+ 3	7	2	7− 8	1

53

7+ 3	21× 7	2÷ 2	4	1− 6	5	8 8	6× 1
4	3	224× 8	2− 5	7	4× 2	1	6
1− 5	4− 6	4	7	64× 8	1	2	14+ 3
6	2	25× 5	3÷ 3	1	8	7	4
7− 8	5	1	12× 2	3	10+ 6	4	280× 7
1	4− 4	2÷ 3	6	2	7 7	5	8
5− 2	8	7 7	4÷ 1	4	90× 3	6	5
7	5− 1	6	8 8	9+ 5	4	1− 3	2

54

21+ 6	8	15+ 5	6× 1	18× 3	2	2÷ 4	5− 7
18+ 5	7	4	6	1	3	8	2
8	5	6	80× 2	4	49× 7	3 3	5− 1
2÷ 4	12+ 3	8	5	2	1	7	6
2	1	28× 7	4	1− 8	20× 5	3÷ 6	3 3
2÷ 3	6	7− 1	8	7	4	2	20× 5
8+ 1	2 2	9+ 3	13+ 7	6	3− 8	5	4
7	4	2	3 3	11+ 5	6	7− 1	8

55

(7) 7	(3+) 1	2	(20×) 5	(1−) 8	(2÷) 6	3	(24×) 4
(3÷) 6	(15+) 8	1	4	7	(75×) 5	2	3
2	7	(2÷) 4	8	(5×) 1	3	5	(3÷) 6
(13+) 4	3	(3−) 8	(3÷) 6	5	1	(7) 7	2
(48×) 3	6	5	2	(168×) 4	(7−) 8	1	(7) 7
8	2	(21×) 3	1	6	7	(10+) 4	(40×) 5
(4−) 1	(1−) 5	7	(3) 3	(2÷) 2	4	6	8
5	4	(6) 6	(4−) 7	3	(4÷) 2	8	1

56

(15×) 3	(8+) 7	(2÷) 2	4	(1−) 5	(15+) 8	(5−) 6	1
5	1	(4−) 3	(8) 8	6	7	(2−) 2	4
(6+) 1	5	7	(8+) 3	(2÷) 2	4	(48×) 8	6
(2÷) 4	(36×) 6	1	5	(15+) 8	(10+) 2	3	(7) 7
8	(128×) 4	6	(9+) 2	7	5	(4−) 1	(1−) 3
(84×) 6	8	4	7	(12×) 1	(3) 3	5	2
7	2	(4−) 5	1	3	(6×) 6	(160×) 4	8
(6×) 2	3	(2−) 8	6	4	1	(7) 7	5

57

(15×) 3	(15+) 7	(96×) 8	4	(3÷) 6	(6+) 5	(2÷) 2	1
5	8	(4) 4	3	2	1	(336×) 7	6
(4÷) 2	(10+) 1	(15+) 7	5	3	(10+) 4	6	8
8	3	6	(3÷) 2	(2÷) 4	(5−) 7	(4−) 1	5
(9+) 1	5	3	6	8	2	(3−) 4	7
(17+) 7	4	(3+) 1	(3−) 8	5	(2÷) 6	3	(2) 2
(4) 4	6	2	(35×) 7	(7−) 1	8	(12+) 5	3
(3÷) 6	2	5	1	(7) 7	(24×) 3	8	4

58

(2−) 6	8	(2÷) 3	(12+) 5	4	(3+) 1	2	(10+) 7
(4−) 8	4	6	(17+) 7	3	(10×) 5	1	2
(18+) 5	6	(8) 8	3	7	2	(4÷) 4	1
7	(6+) 1	(11+) 4	(4÷) 8	2	(3) 3	(90×) 6	5
(2÷) 2	5	7	(2×) 1	(48×) 6	8	3	(4) 4
4	(10+) 3	5	2	1	(210×) 7	(2−) 8	6
(3÷) 3	2	(2÷) 1	(2−) 4	5	6	(2−) 7	(11+) 8
1	(7) 7	2	6	(2÷) 8	4	5	3

59

(13+) 8	3	2	(2−) 7	(2−) 6	(1−) 5	(4×) 1	4
(1−) 2	(15+) 8	7	5	4	6	(7+) 3	1
3	(19+) 5	6	8	(3+) 2	1	4	(2−) 7
(2−) 4	6	(8) 8	(3+) 1	(42×) 3	7	2	5
(49×) 1	7	(60×) 4	2	(64×) 8	(90×) 3	5	6
7	(3+) 2	5	(4) 4	1	8	(2÷) 6	3
(11+) 5	1	3	(13+) 6	7	(4) 4	(4÷) 8	2
6	(4) 4	(3÷) 1	3	(7+) 5	2	(1−) 7	8

60

(4−) 5	1	(8) 8	(14+) 4	(3÷) 6	2	(84×) 7	3
(15+) 8	2	5	6	3	1	4	(6−) 7
(12+) 7	5	(2÷) 2	(4−) 8	4	(18+) 6	3	1
(3÷) 1	3	4	(7+) 5	(560×) 8	7	2	(11+) 6
(17+) 4	(2÷) 6	3	2	7	(7−) 8	1	5
3	4	(49×) 1	7	2	5	(16+) 6	8
6	(672×) 8	7	(3) 3	(5×) 1	(12+) 4	5	2
2	7	6	1	5	3	(2÷) 8	4

61

1− 4	2− 5	2÷ 1	2	4− 7	3	2− 8	6
3	7	192× 4	10+ 6	3+ 2	35× 5	7− 1	8
6− 2	6	8	3	1	7	480× 4	3− 5
8	10+ 3	7	1	4	6	5	2
13+ 5	8	7+ 3	4	19+ 6	2	84× 7	6− 1
3+ 1	2	210× 6	5	8	4	3	7
168× 6	1	80× 5	7	3	6− 8	2	1− 4
7	4	2	8	5 5	6× 1	6	3

62

2− 6	8	7− 1	14+ 7	2÷ 4	2	2− 5	3
3÷ 1	4− 6	8	4	3	35× 7	2÷ 2	80× 5
3	2	1− 7	6	1	5	4	8
40× 4	5	72× 3	64× 1	8	42× 6	7	2
2	4	6	8	2− 5	3	1	8+ 7
40× 5	3− 7	4	17+ 2	6	7− 8	2÷ 3	1
8	6× 3	2	2− 5	7	1	6	10+ 4
8+ 7	1	5 5	3	2	4− 4	8	6

63

5− 2	7	2÷ 8	4	4− 5	1	2÷ 6	3
1− 6	7− 1	84× 7	10+ 5	3	7+ 2	17+ 8	4
7	8	3	2	1	4	5	20+ 6
2÷ 1	2	4	16+ 7	288× 8	6	24× 3	5
1− 4	5	1	8	6	5− 3	2	7
96× 3	1− 6	5	6− 1	7	8	4	2
8	4	36× 6	3	2	5 5	49× 7	7− 1
30× 5	3	2	2− 6	4	7	1	8

64

11+ 3	21+ 7	8	1	5	18+ 2	6	16× 4
7	15+ 8	2	2− 5	3	6	4	1
1	5	90× 6	56× 8	7	4	42× 2	3
1− 6	2− 4	5	3	3+ 2	7− 8	1	7
5	6	3− 4	7	1	16+ 3	13+ 8	4÷ 2
4 4	6× 3	4− 7	2÷ 2	2− 6	1	5	8
4÷ 2	1	3	4	8	5	4− 7	1− 6
8	2	6× 1	6	4 4	7	3	5

65

2240× 5	8	2	7	4	14+ 1	108× 6	3
84× 4	3	7	2 2	5	8	15+ 1	6
1− 6	7	1− 4	5	20+ 2	3	8	1
7− 8	3+ 2	1	12+ 4	7	2÷ 6	3	5
1	15+ 6	5	3	8	28× 7	4	2÷ 2
4− 3	5	2− 8	6	10+ 1	2	7	4
7	4	2÷ 6	7− 1	2− 3	5	7+ 2	1− 8
3+ 2	1	3	8	10+ 6	4	5	7

66

18+ 6	2÷ 2	1	4 4	7− 8	8+ 3	5	4− 7
2	256× 4	8	25× 5	1	13+ 6	7	3
3	8	5	1	1− 6	7	16× 4	2
7	14+ 5	6	24+ 8	3	3− 1	2	4 4
1− 5	3	14× 2	6	7	4	48× 1	8
4	1	7	18+ 2	5	5− 8	3	6
7− 1	20+ 6	3	7	4	6− 2	8	4− 5
8	7	4	1− 3	2	1− 5	6	1

67

5− 3	2− 4	15+ 8	2− 7	5	3÷ 2	6	9+ 1
8	6	7	2÷ 2	1	19+ 4	5	3
48× 4	3− 2	5	9× 3	7	8	3+ 1	18+ 6
6	224× 8	4	1	3	16+ 5	2	7
2	7	1	10+ 4	6	3	8	5
6+ 1	5	2÷ 3	6	2÷ 8	7 7	2÷ 4	2
13+ 7	1	4− 2	15+ 5	4	5− 6	5− 3	8
5	3 3	6	8	2	1	28× 7	4

68

11+ 3	3÷ 6	2	23+ 7	8	40× 4	5	1 1
6	48× 3	4	4− 5	1	7	2	5− 8
2	4	56× 8	1	210× 6	5	7	3
17+ 4	5	7	3÷ 6	4− 3	7− 8	1	24× 2
7− 1	8	15× 5	2	7	12× 6	3	4
8	2 2	3	13+ 4	5	1	960× 6	1− 7
2− 5	9+ 7	1	17+ 3	4	2	8	6
7	1	6	8	1− 2	3	4	5

69

21+ 8	6	7	120× 3	2− 2	4	4− 1	5
11+ 4	1	5	8	12+ 7	3	2÷ 6	2− 2
1	5	21+ 6	7	8	2	3	4
12+ 3	1− 7	8	12× 2	6	1− 5	12× 4	1
7	2	1− 4	5	1	6	80× 8	3
14+ 6	4÷ 8	2	11+ 4	3	6− 1	5	15+ 7
5	3	5− 1	6	4	7	2	8
2÷ 2	4	15× 3	1	5	336× 8	7	6

70

9+ 1	1− 8	4÷ 4	12+ 7	5	24× 3	2	11+ 6
8	7	1	30× 2	3	4	2÷ 6	5
1− 4	14+ 1	2	5	1− 7	6	3	4− 8
3	6	5	7− 1	8	3− 2	49× 7	4
2÷ 6	3	64× 8	4	2	5	1	7
2− 2	4	48× 6	8	24× 1	2− 7	5	2− 3
20+ 5	5− 2	7	2÷ 3	6	4− 8	4	1
7	5	3	6	4	1	6− 8	2

71

2− 4	6	11+ 3	8	2− 7	5	2÷ 2	1
140× 7	4	4÷ 8	2	192× 6	3× 1	3	7+ 5
5	168× 7	3÷ 6	15+ 3	4	8	1	2
3	8	2	6	1	16+ 7	5	4
14+ 6	2÷ 2	4	1	3− 5	1− 3	15+ 8	7
8	3÷ 3	1	5	2	4	22+ 7	6
2÷ 1	11+ 5	11+ 7	4	168× 8	4− 2	6	3
2	1	5	7	3	6	4− 4	8

72

8+ 1	6× 2	3	2− 6	8	18+ 7	5	4− 4
7	60× 5	4	3	2÷ 2	1	6	8
11+ 5	8× 4	1	4− 7	3	2− 6	6− 8	2
4	6− 1	2	2− 5	7	8	2÷ 3	6
2	7	7− 8	1	5− 6	80× 5	4	10+ 3
3− 3	6	3− 5	8	1	4	2÷ 2	7
144× 6	56× 8	7	40× 2	4	42× 3	1	6+ 5
8	3	10+ 6	4	5	2	7	1

73

18+ 8	3	2÷ 2	1	12+ 7	5	144× 6	4
7	5− 2	240× 5	6	8	7+ 3	4	1
3− 2	7	48× 1	1− 3	16× 4	280× 8	5	6
5	8	6	2	1	4	7	15× 3
2− 4	6	3− 7	16+ 8	3	12× 2	1	5
2− 3	1	4	12+ 7	5	6	1− 2	1− 8
6 6	4− 4	8	5	3÷ 2	6− 1	3	7
4− 1	5	1− 3	4	6	7	4÷ 8	2

74

2÷ 2	9+ 7	56× 8	48× 3	9+ 5	4	5− 1	6
1	2	7	8	1008× 6	1− 5	4	3 3
96× 3	1− 4	5	2	8	14+ 6	7	1
4	1	1− 6	5	3	7	3÷ 2	1− 8
8	5 5	14+ 3	4	7+ 1	30× 2	6	7
16+ 6	7− 8	1	7	4	3	5	3− 2
7	3	2− 4	6	2	8× 1	8	5
13+ 5	6	2	6− 1	7	15+ 8	3	4

75

1− 4	42× 3	7	13+ 6	1− 5	7− 8	1	1− 2
3	17+ 6	2	7	4	4− 5	4− 8	1
1− 8	5	6	1− 3	2	1	4	12+ 7
7	12+ 4	192× 8	2	3÷ 1	3	1− 6	5
2 2	1	3	4	2÷ 6	3− 7	5	96× 8
30× 5	7	4− 1	7− 8	3	4	2	6
6	64× 8	5	1	20+ 7	18+ 2	3	1− 4
1	2	4	5	8	6	7	3

76

30× 5	6	17+ 8	9	18+ 7	4÷ 1	4	7+ 3	3− 2
3÷ 1	7− 9	2	3	8	6 6	35× 7	4	5
3	180× 4	9	7− 8	1− 2	56× 7	5	13+ 6	1 1
3÷ 6	2	5	1	3	8	162× 9	7	3− 4
280× 8	5	2− 4	6	8− 1	9	3	2 2	7
7	8× 8	3+ 1	2	45× 5	7+ 4	6	18+ 9	3
2 2	1	3− 7	4	9	3	3− 8	5	6
5− 9	4− 3	14+ 6	140× 7	4	5	3+ 2	1	576× 8
4	7	3	5	6 6	3+ 2	1	8	9

77

18+ 3	8	10+ 6	4	3+ 1	2	2− 7	11+ 5	63× 9
4	3	2 2	56× 7	8	17+ 9	5	6	1
90× 6	5	3	3+ 1	2	8	9 9	36× 4	7
63× 7	3− 4	2÷ 8	3÷ 6	9 9	30× 5	3+ 2	1	3
9	7	4	2	30× 5	6	1	3	2÷ 8
15+ 5	8− 9	1	2− 3	6	112× 7	8	2	4
8	2	2− 9	5	9× 3	1	2− 4	13+ 7	6
2× 2	1	7	72× 9	11+ 4	3	6	8 8	10× 5
1	1− 6	5	8	7	4 4	6− 3	9	2

78

6× 3	7− 1	8	9+ 7	2	800× 5	8− 9	4 4	15+ 6
2	63× 9	7	60× 5	4	8	1	6	3
8− 1	7− 2	9	3	5	4	18+ 6	7	64× 8
9	5− 3	2÷ 2	4	13+ 6	7 7	5	8	1
3− 4	8	14+ 5	9	7	5− 6	1− 3	4× 1	2
7	2− 5	3	3÷ 6	8× 8	1	4	2	315× 9
17+ 5	6 6	10+ 4	2	1	17+ 9	8	3÷ 3	7
8	4	6	3÷ 1	3	1− 2	7 7	9	5
1− 6	7	1 1	17+ 8	9	3	11+ 2	5	4

79

210× 6	5	224× 7	15+ 4	9	4÷ 2	8	9× 1	3
3+ 1	7	4	2	56× 8	3− 6	9	3	5 5
2	4÷ 4	8	17+ 9	7	2− 5	6× 3	36× 6	1
13+ 9	1	17+ 3	8	5 5	7	2	224× 4	6
4	6 6	5	36× 3	2	8− 9	1	7	8
2− 5	3	9	6	3× 1	4 4	3− 7	4÷ 8	18× 2
1− 7	8	17+ 6	5 5	3	1	4	2	9
5− 3	9	2	6− 1	12+ 4	8	1− 6	12+ 5	7
8	3+ 2	1	7	2÷ 6	3	5	5− 9	4

80

1− 4	5	1− 3	24× 6	17+ 9	378× 7	4÷ 2	8	13+ 1
1 1	28× 7	2	4	8	6	6− 9	3	5
3÷ 2	4	16+ 8	5	3	9	6 6	8− 1	7
6	17+ 8	21× 7	3	3− 5	2	5× 1	9	4 4
5− 8	9	30× 6	14× 7	3+ 2	1	5	4 4	189× 3
3	4− 6	5	2	1	8 8	16+ 4	7	9
315× 9	2	9× 1	4− 8	4	1− 3	7	5	16+ 6
5	3÷ 3	9	1	1− 7	4	48× 8	6	2
7	1	13+ 4	9	6	30× 5	3	2	8

81

4− 6	2	17+ 9	8	8+ 7	1	1− 4	5	1− 3
8− 1	9	2− 5	1− 3	4÷ 8	6 6	5− 7	2	4
8+ 3	5	7	4	2	15+ 9	6	64× 8	1
22+ 5	1− 3	3÷ 6	2− 7	8− 1	28× 4	2÷ 2	9 9	8
8	4	2	5	9	7	1	126× 3	6 6
9	3× 1	3	36× 2	160× 4	8	5	6	7
28× 4	8 8	1	6	3	1− 2	17+ 9	8+ 7	7+ 5
7	10+ 6	4	8− 9	30× 5	3	8	1	2
2 2	1− 7	8	1	6	15× 5	3	36× 4	9

82

3+ 1	16+ 8	3	16+ 7	4÷ 2	270× 9	5	6	4 4
2	12× 6	5	3	8	3− 7	4	8− 1	9
3÷ 3	1	2	6	13+ 5	8	9 9	72× 4	14× 7
9	225× 5	112× 7	8	16× 1	4	6	3	2
5	9	5− 6	2	4	9+ 1	8	2− 7	5− 3
6 6	14+ 7	1	9+ 4	3− 3	10+ 5	2	9	8
3− 7	4	17+ 9	5	6	2 2	3	7− 8	1
4	3	8	16+ 9	7	126× 6	10× 1	2	5
4÷ 8	2	4 4	8− 1	9	3	7	1− 5	6

83

8− 9	1− 4	5	3+ 1	2	14+ 3	14+ 6	8	1− 7
1	8 8	28× 7	4	9	2	15× 5	3	6
3÷ 6	21× 7	3	20+ 5	4÷ 1	504× 8	9	1− 4	4÷ 2
2	9× 3	6	9	4	7	7− 1	5	8
3	1	2− 4	6	7 7	18+ 5	8	3÷ 2	3÷ 9
4÷ 8	2	1 1	4− 7	40× 5	9	4	6	3
24× 4	6	11+ 9	3	8	2÷ 1	2	2− 7	5 5
17+ 7	5	2	96× 8	6	20+ 4	3 3	9	4× 1
5	72× 9	8	2	3	6	7	1	4

84

105× 3	2 2	14+ 5	9	6× 1	6	224× 4	8	7
5	17+ 8	9	4− 3	7	1	360× 6	2÷ 2	4
7	6× 6	1	21+ 4	9	8 8	5	3	10× 2
7− 2	1	3 3	8	1− 6	16+ 9	7	4	5
9	3− 3	6	7 7	5	1− 4	3+ 2	1	216× 8
13+ 4	9	17+ 7	2	8	5	7− 1	6 6	3
1− 6	7	3+ 2	1	48× 4	21× 3	8	270× 5	9
9+ 1	2÷ 4	8	1− 5	2	7	3÷ 3	9	6
8	1− 5	4	6	3	2	9	8+ 7	1

85

11+ 3	4	360× 8	9	5	1− 6	7	2÷ 2	6− 1
4	11+ 2	9	108× 6	3	320× 5	8	1	7
8− 1	9	1− 2	3	6	8	28× 4	7	5 5
336× 6	5− 8	3	140× 4	7	8− 1	9	90× 5	2
8	7	4 4	5	1− 2	3	5− 1	6	9
3− 2	2− 5	7	14+ 1	2÷ 8	4	2÷ 6	216× 9	3
5	5− 1	6	7	5− 9	11+ 2	3	8	22+ 4
189× 7	6	4− 1	16× 2	4	9	10+ 5	3	8
9	3	5	8	1	7 7	2	4	6

86

8+ 3	16+ 7	8 8	1− 6	5	5− 9	4÷ 2	3− 1	4
5	9	3÷ 3	1	9+ 2	4	8	1− 6	7
13+ 6	25× 5	1	4	3	1− 8	9	13+ 7	144× 2
7	72× 3	5	135× 9	2÷ 1	2	13+ 6	4	8
2÷ 1	4	6	3	3− 8	5	7	2	9
2	4÷ 8	63× 7	5	8− 9	1	72× 4	3	6
8 8	2	9	28× 7	4	630× 6	3	4− 5	3÷ 1
3− 4	1	16× 2	2− 8	6	7	5	9	3
54× 9	6	4	2	21× 7	3	1	3− 8	5

87

11+ 5	6	1− 2	3	18+ 4	8	7 7	18× 9	1
19+ 3	25× 1	5	2÷ 4	8	6	2− 9	7	2
9	5	11+ 4	2	10+ 3	7	4× 1	144× 8	6
7	17+ 8	9	5	3÷ 6	2	4	1	3
2÷ 4	8− 9	1	30× 6	5	5− 3	8	9+ 2	7
2	11+ 7	3÷ 3	1	10+ 9	120× 5	6	4	1440× 8
5− 6	4	56× 7	8	1	7− 9	2	14+ 3	5
1	5− 3	8	2− 7	2− 2	4	9+ 5	6	9
16+ 8	2	6	9	7 7	1	3	5	4

88

192× 6	8	21+ 7	3	2	8− 9	1	1− 4	5
4	10+ 7	9	4× 2	5− 6	1	8+ 5	3	21+ 8
17+ 9	3	2	1	112× 4	7	3− 8	5	6
8	30× 1	5	13+ 9	9× 3	4	84× 2	6	7
3− 2	5	6	4	1	3	7	1− 8	9
2÷ 1	2	1− 4	5	1− 8	270× 6	9	4− 7	3
378× 7	6	5− 3	8	9	5	24× 4	16× 1	2
2− 3	9	1 1	294× 7	3− 5	8	6	2	4
5	4− 4	8	6	7	1− 2	3	8− 9	1

89

216× 6	8− 1	9	17+ 2	8	3− 7	4	2− 3	5
4	4− 9	21+ 5	7	3+ 1	2	64× 8	36× 6	3
9	5	7	3	6	12× 4	1	8	2
6× 1	6	80× 2	17+ 8	9	3	1− 5	4	1− 7
2− 7	4÷ 2	8	5	108× 4	9	3	8+ 1	6
5	8	3− 1	4	3− 3	6	84× 2	7	17+ 9
6− 2	12× 3	24× 4	6	25× 5	1	7	7− 9	8
8	4	3− 3	8− 9	9+ 7	5	6	2	4÷ 1
21× 3	7	6	1	2	22+ 8	9	5	4

90

15+ 2	6	7	3÷ 9	3	2− 5	1− 8	4× 4	1
26+ 4	9	80× 8	5	2	3	7	1	6 6
5	8	10+ 1	3	6	90× 9	2	17+ 7	4
17+ 9	12× 3	4	42× 7	21+ 1	3+ 2	5	6	13+ 8
8	2÷ 4	2	6	7	1	6− 3	7− 9	5
1 1	49× 7	3− 6	8	5	2÷ 4	9	2	14+ 3
7	1	3	4÷ 4	17+ 9	8	2− 6	15× 5	2
2÷ 6	3− 2	4− 5	1	8	14+ 7	4	3	9
3	5	9	2÷ 2	4	6	1	1− 8	7

91

16+ 7	1− 8	225× 9	5	9× 3	6 6	2÷ 2	1	14+ 4
4	9	5	63× 7	1	3	4− 6	2	8
5	2− 6	8	9	252× 4	1− 7	3÷ 1	3	2
3÷ 1	2− 7	4− 2	6	9	8	360× 5	4	3
3	5	4÷ 1	4	7	40× 2	17+ 9	8	6
6− 9	3	168× 6	5− 8	3÷ 2	5	4	12+ 7	8+ 1
2÷ 2	1	4	3	6	17+ 9	8	5	7
96× 8	2	7	1	20× 5	4	4− 3	3− 6	4− 9
6	192× 4	3	2	8	1	7	9	5

92

9 9	16× 4	3+ 1	2	1− 8	7	11+ 5	3	90× 6
4	1	1− 8	3− 7	7− 9	2	3	36× 6	5
1− 7	8	9	4	10× 2	5	6	1	3
30× 1	6	24× 3	8	16+ 7	18+ 4	9	5	7− 2
2− 8	5	48× 6	3÷ 1	4	13+ 3	2	441× 7	9
6	2	4	3	5	1 1	8	9	7
7− 2	9	2− 7	5	2÷ 3	6	3− 1	4	256× 8
11+ 5	3	108× 2	6	8− 1	9	3− 7	8	4
3	35× 7	5	9	2− 6	8	4	2÷ 2	1

93

3÷ 9	40× 5	4	2	2− 6	24× 1	3	8	3− 7
3	20+ 9	5− 6	1	8	6− 2	12+ 5	7	4
6	3	2	8+ 7	1	8	3− 9	4÷ 4	8+ 5
15+ 8	2	2− 7	9	4 4	360× 5	6	1	3
1	20+ 7	5	2÷ 4	2	9	8	2− 3	3÷ 6
4	8	432× 9	6	21× 3	7	56× 1	5	2
3+ 2	1	8	11+ 3	2− 5	10+ 4	7	3− 6	8− 9
20× 5	4	3÷ 3	8	7	6	2	9	1
13+ 7	6	1	17+ 5	9	3	4	4÷ 2	8

94

48× 8	6	3− 4	7	3 3	45× 1	5	26+ 9	2
105× 3	19+ 2	12+ 5	6	4÷ 1	4	9	7	8
7	8	1	7− 9	2	1− 6	1− 4	3	5 5
5	9	2− 6	4÷ 2	8	7	3÷ 3	1	2− 4
24× 1	4− 7	8	17+ 3	5	9	2÷ 2	20× 4	6
4	3	56× 7	8	4− 6	2	1	5	8− 9
6	10× 5	2	252× 4	9	8+ 3	56× 7	2− 8	1
2÷ 2	4	8− 9	1	7	5	8	6	4− 3
13+ 9	1	3	17+ 5	4	8	4− 6	2	7

95

4− 7	15+ 9	14+ 2	8	4	9+ 1	6	5 5	15× 3
3	6	12+ 4	1	6− 9	2	1− 8	7	5
9 9	17+ 4	7	24× 6	3	22+ 5	16× 1	8	2
1	7	5	4	8	9	4− 3	1− 2	5− 6
2÷ 2	6+ 5	17+ 8	9	17+ 6	4	7	3	1
4	1	3÷ 6	2	7	8+ 3	5	72× 9	8
3840× 5	2	27× 9	3	1	4− 8	4	1− 6	7
6	8	9× 3	70× 5	2	2− 7	9	7+ 1	13+ 4
8	3	1	7	1− 5	6	2	4	9

96

12× 3	4	10+ 7	7+ 2	4− 5	1	25+ 8	3− 9	6
2÷ 4	14× 2	3	5	9	7	1	14+ 6	8
8	7	864× 9	2÷ 1	2	7+ 5	2− 6	4	3÷ 3
5 5	8	6	3÷ 3	1	2	28× 4	7	9
8− 9	1	2	22+ 4	3	6	3− 5	8	9+ 7
14+ 1	15× 3	4÷ 4	14+ 8	6	9	2− 7	5	2
6	5	1	9 9	224× 7	8	6+ 3	2	20× 4
7	108× 9	240× 8	6	4	9+ 3	2	1	5
2	6	5	1− 7	8	4	6− 9	3	1

97

30× 3	17+ 4	9	16× 8	8+ 2	5	1	42× 6	7
5	2	4	1	18+ 3	7	6 6	108× 9	2− 8
20+ 7	8− 9	1	2	5 5	8	3	4	6
9	4− 5	1− 8	23+ 7	1	2÷ 6	2÷ 4	2	1− 3
4	1	7	9	6	3	400× 8	5	2
39+ 8	6	5	4	7	9	2	3÷ 3	1
9+ 2	20+ 8	3	11+ 6	4	1	5	2− 7	9
6	7	2	25+ 3	8	36× 4	9	10+ 1	5
1	2÷ 3	6	5	9	112× 2	7	8	4

98

5− 9	17+ 2	3	2÷ 8	4	11+ 5	27× 1	42× 6	7
4	7	5	2÷ 1	2	6	3	9	2÷ 8
6− 3	9	32× 1	3÷ 2	6	56× 8	16+ 5	7 7	4
3− 5	8	4	2− 3	1	7	9	2	3÷ 6
7+ 1	6	8	21+ 9	216× 3	4	18+ 7	5	2
2− 8	4− 1	7	5	9	2	6	7+ 4	3÷ 3
6	5	2÷ 2	4	2− 7	24× 1	8	3	9
3− 7	4	3− 9	6	5	3	72× 2	7− 8	1
1− 2	3	21+ 6	7	8	9	4	6+ 1	5

99

11+ 6	2÷ 2	6− 1	7	16+ 9	3	3− 8	15+ 5	4
3	1	360× 8	3− 9	4	12+ 2	5	6	7 7
2	672× 7	9	6	1	5	4	24× 3	8
4	6	5	144× 8	3	504× 9	9+ 2	7	1
24+ 9	4	9× 3	1	6	8	7	3− 2	5
5	9	24× 4	3	1400× 8	22+ 7	6	1− 1	2
1	3	2	5	7	4÷ 4	9	2÷ 8	3− 6
1− 7	8	3÷ 6	2	5	1	3÷ 3	4	9
40× 8	5	3− 7	4	4− 2	6	1	6− 9	3

100

4− 5	1	5− 9	4	126× 6	3	7	4÷ 2	13+ 8
17+ 4	21× 3	7	20× 5	2	15+ 6	9	8	1
7	6	13+ 3	2	1− 8	9	5+ 1	20× 5	4
4÷ 8	2	6	1890× 7	5	1	3	4	9 9
9+ 2	17+ 8	4	6	9	112× 7	16+ 5	1	3
6	9	17+ 5	36× 1	4	2	8	4− 3	7
1	4	8	9	30× 3	5	2	7	1− 6
3÷ 9	2− 7	6+ 2	3	1	4− 8	2− 4	6	5
3	5	16+ 1	8	7	4	17+ 6	9	2